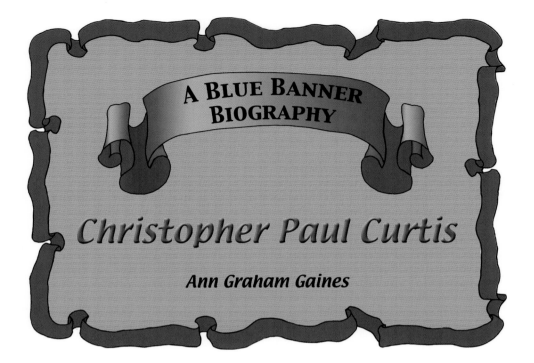

A BLUE BANNER BIOGRAPHY

Christopher Paul Curtis

Ann Graham Gaines

Mitchell Lane
PUBLISHERS

P.O. Box 196
Hockessin, Delaware 19707
Visit us on the web: www.mitchelllane.com
Comments? email us: mitchelllane@mitchelllane.com

Printing   2   3   4   5   6   7   8   9

Blue Banner Biographies

Alicia Keys	Allen Iverson	Allen Jackson
Ashanti	Ashlee Simpson	Ashton Kutcher
Avril Lavigne	Beyoncé	Bow Wow
Britney Spears	Christina Aguilera	**Christopher Paul Curtis**
Clay Aiken	Condoleezza Rice	Daniel Radcliffe
Derek Jeter	Eminem	Eve
Gwen Stefani	Ice Cube	Ja Rule
Jay-Z	Jennifer Lopez	J. K. Rowling
Jodie Foster	Justin Berfield	Kate Hudson
Kelly Clarkson	Kenny Chesney	Lance Armstrong
Lee Ann Womack	Lindsay Lohan	Mariah Carey
Mario	Mary-Kate and Ashley Olsen	Melissa Gilbert
Michael Jackson	Miguel Tejada	Missy Elliott
Nelly	Orlando Bloom	P. Diddy
Paris Hilton	Peyton Manning	Queen Latifah
Rita Williams-Garcia	Ritchie Valens	Ron Howard
Rudy Giuliani	Sally Field	Selena
Shirley Temple	Tim McGraw	Usher

Library of Congress Cataloging-in-Publication Data
Gaines, Ann.
    Christopher Paul Curtis / Ann Graham Gaines.
       p. cm. — (A blue banner biography)
    Includes bibliographical references and index.
    ISBN 1-58415-330-X (lib. bound)
    1. Curtis, Christopher Paul—Juvenile literature. 2. Authors, American—20th century—Biography—Juvenile literature. 3. African American authors—Biography—Juvenile literature. 4. Children's stories—Authorship—Juvenile literature. I. Title. II. Series.
PS3553.U6944Z68 2005
813'.54—dc22

2004021876
ISBN-10: 1-58415-330-X   ISBN-13: 978-158415-330-6

ABOUT THE AUTHOR: Ann Graham Gaines holds a graduate degree in American Civilization and Library and Information Science from the University of Texas at Austin. She has been a freelance writer for 20 years, specializing in nonfiction for children. She lives near Gonzales, Texas, with her husband and their four children.

PHOTO CREDITS: Cover, p. 4 James Keyser/Random House Books; p. 6 The Flint Journal; p. 12 Associated Press; p. 21 Tanga Morris; p. 24 Gloria Coles/Flint Public Library; p. 28 Tanga Morris.

PUBLISHER'S NOTE: The following story has been thoroughly researched, and to the best of our knowledge, represents a true story. While every possible effort has been made to ensure accuracy, the publisher will not assume liability for damages caused by inaccuracies in the data, and makes no warranty on the accuracy of the information contained herein. This story has not been authorized or endorsed by Christopher Paul Curtis.

PCG 2-28-29-30

CONTENTS

Christopher Paul Curtis is an award-winning author. He has received the Newbery Medal and the Coretta Scott King Award.

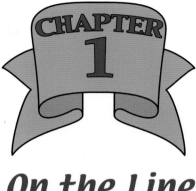

On the Line

*T*oday Christopher Paul Curtis is a famous author. He is one of the few African Americans who has ever won the Newbery Medal, the most important award given to a children's book. But he has not been an author for very long.

When he was a young man, he had a different job that was much less fulfilling. He worked on the assembly line in an automobile factory in Flint, Michigan. Flint is close to Detroit, which is considered the center of the U.S. automobile industry. For thirteen years, day after day after day after day, he hung doors on car bodies as they came down the line. The work paid extremely well, but it was very boring. The job didn't require any special skills and it never presented a challenge.

Curtis and a friend he had made on the assembly line took turns hanging doors. When a car came down the line, Curtis would work on it. When the next car arrived, his friend handled it. They switched back and forth like this all day.

This is the Fisher Auto Body Plant where Curtis worked for many years.

Finally the two men made a deal and changed their routine. Instead of working for two or three minutes to hang a door and then taking two or three minutes off while the other man took over, each man would work straight for half an hour at a time. Curtis would hang every door for thirty minutes while his buddy took time off. Then he switched with the other man and he had half an hour to do as he pleased.

What pleased Curtis was writing in a journal to record his thoughts. He had always enjoyed writing. Now writing helped him escape from the boredom and the banging and clanging of huge machines. When Curtis wrote, he could tune the noise out. He also found himself feeling less bored, not just while he was at work, but in his free time, too.

What pleased Curtis was writing in a journal to record his thoughts. He had always enjoyed writing.

These were great benefits. But writing at work also paid off for Curtis in another way. It gave him practice writing. Today, he goes to lots of schools and libraries to talk to children about his books. A happy man who laughs a lot, he likes to encourage other people to try their hand at writing. He tells the story of how he got his own start in writing. He makes sure everybody understands that his first tries at fiction weren't very good. And then he reveals what he believes to be the secret of good writing: Based on his own experience, he says it is practice. Practice. Practice.

> *Curtis's first tries at fiction weren't very good. He believes the secret of good writing is practice.*

Childhood

Christopher Paul Curtis was born in Flint, Michigan on May 10, 1953, to Herman and Leslie Curtis. He was one of five children.

Herman and Leslie were strict and provided their children with a lot of structure by setting many rules they expected them to follow. The parents also gave their children one of the greatest gifts of all, their time. Everyone spent a lot of time together. The Curtises went to family reunions where they heard stories about the rest of their family, especially their grandfathers.

For many years, this country was segregated, which meant that African Americans were forced to go to separate schools and churches, even shop at different stores than white people. Job opportunities were severely limited for black men. So Leslie's father had worked for years as a redcap, loading passengers' luggage onto trains. As a young man, he had also been a professional baseball player, a pitcher for teams in the Negro Baseball League. Jackie Robinson would become the first African American allowed to play baseball with white players in 1947.

Curtis' other grandfather (his father's father) worked during the day painting cars. At night he was a band leader. His most memorable group was the Dusky Devastators of the Depression. He was also among the first African Americans to earn a pilot's license, meaning he could fly a plane.

> **Curtis's grandfather was among the first African Americans to earn a pilot's license.**

The Curtis children were influenced not only by their family, but also by their community. They grew up in an all-black neighborhood. Christopher and his siblings would have white teachers and see white people on television. But like other African Americans living in Flint, they belonged to an isolated group.

Herman Curtis worked as a chiropodist—a foot doctor—when Christopher was born. But Mr. Curtis's patients were all black people and many were too poor to pay him. Sadly, he had to admit he could not support his family as a chiropodist. He gave up his small medical practice to go to work in Flint's Fisher Body plant because the job at the factory paid more.

Leslie Curtis, Christopher's mother, was different from most women in their neighborhood because she had been to college and graduated from Michigan State University. While her children were small, she was a housewife.

Curtis was three years old when a strong-willed black woman named Rosa Parks made history.

Christopher Paul Curtis was three years old when a strong-willed black woman named Rosa Parks made history, refusing to give up her seat on a bus to a white man in Montgomery, Alabama. She was arrested because the law actually made it legal for African Americans to be discriminated against!

Racism was less obvious in the northern American cities than in the South, but it still existed.

Soon a civil rights movement spread across the United States. African Americans (and many white people, too) fought for equal rights. Martin Luther King Jr. rose to prominence as a civil rights leader. The civil rights movement achieved many successes, such as the integration of schools in Little Rock, Arkansas in 1957.

In this photograph Rosa Parks is fingerprinted. She was arrested for refusing to give up her seat on a bus to a white man.

Both of Curtis's parents became very involved in the civil rights movement. He remembers as a boy being taken to marches sponsored by the local chapter of the National Association for the Advancement of Colored People. The NAACP members picketed businesses that would accept blacks as customers but refused to hire them.

School seems to have had less influence on Christopher Paul Curtis than his family or community. He always did well in school, thanks in part to the fact that he was a good reader. His parents always loved to read. "Between my parents, they must have read thousands, tens of thousands of books," he has said. He went to the library a lot as a child. But he did not find many books he liked. Asked as a grown-up to name the book that most influenced him as a child, he could not name a single one. "In the 1960s, there were no books that were for, by, or about African Americans," he explained. Instead of books, he read magazines and comic books.

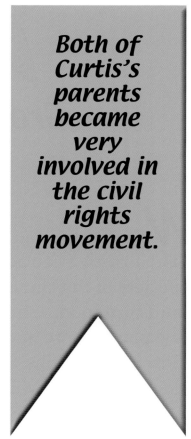

Both of Curtis's parents became very involved in the civil rights movement.

Growing Pains

When Curtis graduated from high school in 1971, he had already been accepted for the following fall as a student at the University of Michigan-Flint. To help him earn money, his father got him a summer job at the plant where he worked. His mother did not want him to take it. She was afraid it would get him off course. And she was right. He did go to college but stayed for only one year. "I did terrible," he later said.

Because he knew he could make good money on the assembly line, college did not seem very important and he soon landed a full-time job at the auto factory. In the years that followed, he would take some college classes, but only on a part-time basis, one or two night classes a year.

Christopher Paul Curtis ended up working on the assembly line for thirteen years. He was stuck in a rut. Over and over again, he performed the same tasks at work. About the only thing he liked about the job was the people he met. A storyteller by nature, he also liked to listen to other people's stories. He found it particularly interesting to listen to stories told by African Americans who had migrated to Flint from the South. They talked about both the good and the bad things they remembered from living there.

> *Curtis ended up working on the assembly line for thirteen years. He was stuck in a rut.*

"The people I lived around always talked very fondly of it, how wonderful it was down home," he told an interviewer. "But there was also this horror of racism hanging over everything." The South had often been the scene of violence. Curtis's parents remembered the days when many blacks were lynched in the South.

In 1978, he went with some friends to see a basketball game in nearby Hamilton, Ontario, located just across from Detroit in Canada. There he met a woman named Kaysandra Sookram. They started to date. Since they lived too far apart to see each other every day, Christopher wrote to her constantly. They eventually were married and had two children, Steven and Cydney. To this day, Kaysandra remembers how lovely his letters were. "I always said those letters should be framed," she said. She told him he could be a writer.

Curtis married Kaysandra Sookram and they had two children, Steven and Cydney.

Married life eased many of Curtis's feelings of dissatisfaction. Because Kaysandra is a nurse, they earned a substantial income. Nevertheless, as time went by, Curtis continued to dream of leaving the factory.

In the early 1990s, he began to think about becoming a writer. He had always liked to read and to write. For years, he had been going to college on a part-time basis. One semester he took a writing class from a professor who was very encouraging. He was keeping his own private journal, too, which helped him to practice writing.

Twice he entered writing contests at the University of Michigan. The first one was an emotional essay that described what happened one day when he realized how he felt about his job.

After work was over that day, he and a huge group of people from his shift emerged from the big, stuffy, noisy building. They waited at a corner for the stoplight to change so they could get their cars and go home. The light turned green. Everybody started to cross the street but Curtis just stood still. He had suddenly been hit by an immense amazement that he had been doing this for thirteen years.

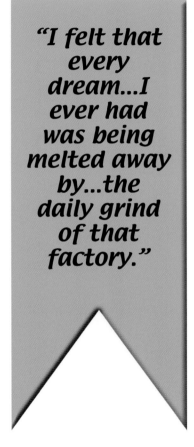

"I felt that every dream...I ever had was being melted away by...the daily grind of that factory."

"I felt that every dream, every hope, every talent I ever had was being melted away by the numbing horror, the endless repetition, the daily grind of that factory," he wrote. He stood there, thinking this awful thought, feeling this terrible feeling, as more and more people passed him.

Finally his friend Muley found him. Muley instantly knew Curtis needed help just to go forward. So Muley steered him across the street and they went to Curtis' car. Muley said to him, "If I was you, I wouldn't come in tomorrow. I know how you feel, some of the time it's just too much, isn't it?"

The judges felt Curtis's essay summed up the feelings of many working men and women.

But Curtis summed up things differently. "I had to agree, it had become too much, but more importantly it had become too little, it had become nothing," he wrote.

That essay won the Avery Hopwood Prize. The judges felt that it summed up the feelings of many working men and women.

What he submitted to the second contest was different. For years, he had tried to write fiction, but never particularly liked what he wrote. But as he approached the age of 40, he began to think he could write stories, too, as well as autobiographical pieces. One vacation, his family decided to go to Florida to visit one of Kaysandra's relatives. The more he thought about the long drive, the more excited Curtis became. He eventually wrote a story about a family like his taking a trip.

It was so good that Curtis won the University of Michigan's Jules Hopwood Prize. He began to think about expanding it. In 1993, his wife made this idea reality when she suggested he leave his job for an entire year so he could make his idea into a book. As a skilled nurse, she made enough money to support the family on her own for a time.

As a skilled nurse Kaysandra made enough money to support the family on her own for a time.

Over the next year, he wrote faithfully day after day on what would become a novel aimed at young readers entitled *The Watsons Go to Birmingham - 1963*. It revolved around a working class, African American family like his. He set his novel during his childhood. But it evolved into much more than a story based on his own experiences. All along, Curtis made the story revolve around the family's vacation. For a long time, his characters also went to Florida.

But he got stuck. He could not figure out what they should do once they arrived in Florida. Then one day his son Steven came home from school, excited about having read a poem called "The Ballad of Birmingham" by Dudley Randall. Interested in African American history, Curtis realized that the church bombing that took place in Birmingham, Alabama in 1963, killing small black girls, would make a compelling story. So he sent the Watsons there instead. The result was what began as a funny book changed into a tragedy, as his characters not only witnessed the bombing, but were victims of it.

Finally he finished *The Watsons*. At first he wondered what to do with it. He knew that most books like the one he had written were handled by agents, who represent authors and present their stories to publishers. But it would take time and money to find an agent. So once again Curtis entered a writing contest.

Every year Delacorte Press offers a prize for a first young adult novel. In the summer of 2000, editor Wendy Lamb still remembered what she thought

> *Finally he finished The Watsons. At first he wondered what to do with it. He decided to enter a writing contest.*

when she opened Curtis's envelope in January 1994.
She knew that a black church had been bombed in
Birmingham in 1963 so immediately recognized what
his book must be about. His very title "filled me with
curiosity and dread. Well, I thought this person was
ambitious, trying to write about something terrible,
something important." She put it aside for a special
look later. What amazed her when she finally read it
was that the book was more than important. It was
also funny and it rang true.

Curtis's second book **Bud, Not Buddy** *won two important awards:
the Newbery Medal and the Coretta Scott King Award. This photo
was taken at one of his award ceremonies.*

Curtis did not win the Delacorte prize. His narrator was too young for a young adult book. And it was classified as historical fiction. But Delacorte wanted to publish his novel anyway. The company gave him an initial advance of $4,000 and promised to pay him royalties if the book sold enough copies.

> When it appeared, it received praise from important critics like one from The New York Times.

When it appeared, it received praise from important critics like one from *The New York Times.* It also won a Newbery Honor, which the American Library Association gives to notable children's books each year, and was named one of the year's best books by the Coretta Scott King Foundation. Over time, it would sell more than 200,000 copies and net Curtis thousands upon thousands of dollars.

Whoopi Goldberg bought the movie rights. LeVar Burton, star of *Roots* and *Star Trek Voyager* and host of PBS's *Reading Rainbow*, agreed to direct the movie. Goldberg will star in it, along with Damon Wayans.

Bud, Not Buddy

By the time *The Watsons* actually appeared in print, Curtis had left his auto factory job. He worked in a different factory, was a customer service representative, and then a maintenance man.

But finally he realized he could be a writer full-time. Delacorte offered him advances to write two more books. He and his family moved to Windsor, Ontario, where his wife works as a nurse in an intensive care unit at a hospital.

Curtis had written *The Watsons* at the Flint Public Library. He went there for a couple of hours every day to write his words by hand on legal pads. At home at night, his son Steven typed his words into the computer. In Windsor, he continued to write the same way. He said he did not like to write on word processors because "They go too fast. With longhand, you think as you're writing. It's a much better pace."

Used to getting up early to go to his factory job, he continued to set his alarm for 5:00 a.m. He'd do some work then, editing what he had written the day before. Then he would help his daughter Cydney get ready for school. By 9:00 he would be seated at a desk in the children's room at the library. He never dreaded going there. He said he knew other writers

Curtis was very happy to make a public appearance at the Flint Public Library. Curtis and his brother often visited the library when they were growing up.

thought their work was difficult. This is not the case for him, however.

"I hear them talk about how hard it is to write, and I feel like a criminal," he said. "It's easy for me to write. I have a riot. I sit in the Windsor library and work and sometimes I just sit there and laugh." Every day he knocked off at noon to go play basketball at the YMCA with friends.

The result was *Bud, Not Buddy*. The story of a boy living in Flint during the Depression in the early 1930s, it was published by Delacorte in 1999. Like *The Watsons*, it is on one level a serious book that deals with huge topics like racism and a person's need to belong to a group. But it is also side-splittingly funny. Bud gets along in life partly because he has a code he lives by.

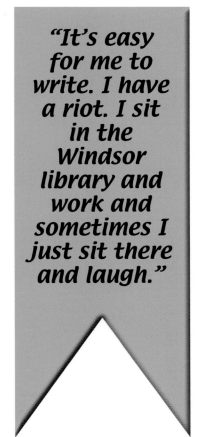

"It's easy for me to write. I have a riot. I sit in the Windsor library and work and sometimes I just sit there and laugh."

This code consists of many "Rules and Things for Having a Funner Life and Making a Better Liar Out of Yourself." Rule number 3 is "If you've got to lie, make sure it's simple and easy to remember." Another example is Number 83, "If an adult tells you not to worry, and you weren't worried before, you better hurry and start 'cause you're already running late."

Curtis was pleased with his book. And it earned good reviews. Still, he was very surprised on the morning of January 17, 2000, when he received two phone calls. The first told him he'd won a Newbery Medal for Children's Literature — the first African American male to receive that honor — which he said is "the equivalent of an Oscar." The Oscars are the awards given every year in Hollywood to the year's best movie, the best actor and actress, and so on. Winning an Oscar virtually guarantees that the actor or actress will have a long and prosperous movie career.

Bud, Not Buddy received the Coretta Scott King Award, named in honor of the widow of slain civil rights leader Martin Luther King, Jr.

Then the second call came. *Bud, Not Buddy* had also received the Coretta Scott King Award, named in honor of the widow of slain civil rights leader Martin Luther King. It is given every year for the outstanding book by a person of African descent.

Looking to
the Future

*B*oth awards led to great increases in the book's sales. Even the smallest libraries order Newbery winners, so Delacorte received orders for at least 100,000 more copies of the book. Because Curtis receives a percentage of every dollar Delacorte makes selling his books, the Newbery meant he earned much more money.

It also gave him great exposure. He appeared on the *Today Show*. He was the subject of an article in *Time* magazine. But his family did not let him get a swelled head. When asked what her father did, his daughter told a reporter what she thought: "Nothing." His wife and his daughter Cydney continue to tease him. One family member says she always knew "by his fibs" that he could be a great writer.

Today Curtis works as a full-time writer. He still writes in longhand. He has contracts for more books. His third book, *Bucking the Sarge,* was published by Wendy Lamb Books in 2004. This book is narrated by 15-year-old Luther and takes place in Flint, Michigan. *Mr. Chickee's Funny Money,* for middle-grade readers, was published in October 2005. It introduces the Flint Future Detectives. According to Curtis, these young sleuths will appear in a series of books.

Curtis photographed at a book signing. Curtis especially loves meeting and talking to children about his writing.

He's also discovered something else he likes about being a popular author. He receives many invitations to sign his books at bookstores. Reporters and writers continue to call and ask for interviews. He also gives many speeches at schools and libraries. All these occasions give him an opportunity to talk, which he loves to do.

In public, he answers questions about himself. He tells audiences he likes to play basketball, collect old records, and eat Mexican, Indian, and West Indian food. He talks to them about books he likes (his favorite authors are Toni Morrison, Kurt Vonnegut, and Zora Neale Hurston). He likes to spin stories and talk about what he has been learning about African American history.

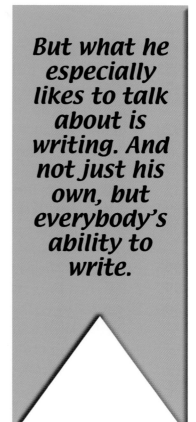

But what he especially likes to talk about is writing. And not just his own, but everybody's ability to write.

But what he especially likes to talk about is writing. And not just his own, but everybody's ability to write. He encourages kids in particular to try all different kinds of writing.

He can hardly wait to get back to his legal pads and on with his stories.

CHRONOLOGY

1953 Born May 10, in Flint, Michigan

1971 Graduates from high school and goes to work at Fisher Body Plant, an automobile factory

1978 Meets his future wife, Kaysandra, at a basketball game in Ontario, Canada

1993 Begins writing full-time as his wife volunteers to support their family for a year

1994 Submits his first novel to a contest sponsored by Delacorte Press. He does not win the prize, but Delacorte wants to publish his book

1995 Publishes *The Watsons Go to Birmingham - 1963*

1999 Publishes *Bud, Not Buddy*

2000 Receives news he has won a Newbery Medal and a Coretta Scott King award, both prizes for an outstanding children's book; receives the IRA Children's Book Award for Older Readers

2001 Receives the Dorothy Canfield Fisher Award and the NMLA Land of Enchantment Book Award; receives the Mayor's Award for Literary Arts (Michigan)

2002 Receives the William Allen White Children's Book Award

2004 Publishes *Bucking the Sarge;* goes on book tour

2005 *Mr. Chickee's Funny Money* is published in October

FOR FURTHER READING

Books:

Curtis, Christopher Paul. *The Watsons Go to Birmingham - 1963.* Delacorte Books for Young Readers, 1995.

Curtis, Christopher Paul. *Bud, Not Buddy.* Delacorte Books for Young Readers, 1999.

Curtis, Christopher Paul. *Bucking the Sarge.* Wendy Lamb Books, 2004.

Websites:

Nothing But Curtis.com

http://christopherpaulcurtis.smartwriters.com/index.2ts

Random House Publishers

http://www.randomhouse.com/features/christopherpaulcurtis/

Children's Book Council

http://www.cbcbooks.org/html/curtislamb.html

Powell.com author interview

http://www.powells.com/authors/curtis.html

Riverbank Review Author Interview

http://www.riverbankreview.com/cpcurtis.html

INDEX